HEALTHY·LIVING·

Talking About

Making
Good Choices

By W. M. Anderson

Gareth Stevens
Publishing

Please visit our Web site **www.garethstevens.com**. For a free color catalog of all our high-quality books, call toll free 1-800-542-2595 or fax 1-877-542-2596.

Library of Congress Cataloging-in-Publication Data

Anderson, W. M. (Wendy M.)
 Talking about making good choices / W.M. Anderson.
     p. cm. -- (Healthy living)
 Includes index.
 ISBN 978-1-4339-3660-9 (library binding)
 1. Health behavior--Juvenile literature. 2. Decision-making--Juvenile literature. I. Title.
 RA776.9.A52 2010
 613--dc22

                              2009043455

Published in 2010 by
Gareth Stevens Publishing
111 East 14th Street, Suite 349
New York, NY 10003

© 2010 Blake Publishing

For Gareth Stevens Publishing:
Art Direction: Haley Harasymiw
Editorial Direction: Kerri O'Donnell

Cover photo: iStockphoto

Photos and illustrations:
pp. 3, 4, 5, 6, 7, 8, 9, 10, 11, 12, 13, 16, 17, 18, 19, 20, 21, 22, 23, 24, 25, 26, 27, 28, 29 (bottom left), 30 iStockphoto; pp. 14, 29 (top and bottom right) Shutterstock.com; p. 15 (top) © Jason Merritt/Getty Images; pp. 15 (bottom), 21 (bottom), 25 (bottom) UC Publishing; pp. 20, 21, 24, 25 Dillon Naylor; p. 28 Photos.com.

Printed in the United States of America

CPSIA compliance information: Batch #CW10GS: For further information contact Gareth Stevens, New York, New York, at 1-800-542-2595.

Contents

Can you make healthy choices?

Our government spends millions of dollars every year to encourage young people to eat healthy foods and lead active lives. That's how important good health choices are. That's how important YOU are!

Eat a balanced diet.

Brush your teeth every morning and night.

The Food Pyramid—a guide to your eating

MyPyramid
STEPS TO A HEALTHIER YOU
MyPyramid.gov

GRAINS | VEGETABLES | FRUITS | MILK | MEAT & BEANS

Check out these Internet sites:

kidshealth.org/kids

www.mypyramid.gov/kids

www.bam.gov

Take this quiz to see how much you already know about making healthy choices.

1 Which statement is correct?

a) You should eat one piece of fruit a day.

b) You should eat two servings of fruit a day.

c) You should only eat fruit if you're a fruit bat.

2 Ten-year-olds need about ten hours of sleep per day. True or false?

3 Regular exercise will help you to:

a) concentrate in school

b) sleep

c) build strong bones and muscles

d) all of the above

4 Having a balanced diet means:

a) resting your plate on your knees while you eat

b) eating a wide variety of foods every day

c) eating three meals a day

d) eating meat, vegetables, and bread

Did you know? A large part of your brain is made up of fat. Your diet affects your brain, moods, and behavior!

5 A healthy diet does not contain fats. True or false?

6 To have an active lifestyle you must:

a) compete in a team sport

b) be busy all the time

c) include at least an hour of physical activity in your daily life

d) give up computer games and television

7 Active children grow up to be active adults. True or false?

8 Adults should choose what's healthy for kids. True or false?

Answers

1 b: You should eat two servings of fruit a day. By the way, half a cup of juice counts as a serving. See how easy it is?

2 True: Ten hours is ideal for somebody of that age. Getting enough sleep helps your brain to work at its best. Your body also repairs itself while you sleep.

3 d: All of the above. Regular exercise rocks!

4 b: Eating a wide variety of foods every day.

5 False: Our bodies need a small amount of fat to work properly.

6 c: Include at least one hour of physical activity in your daily life. Dancing, skating, shooting hoops, walking to school—they can all be part of an active lifestyle.

7 That depends. Some people stop being active. However, active kids are more likely to become active adults.

8 This one's a bit tricky. True, adults should choose what's healthy for kids, but do they always? Isn't it better if kids make healthy choices for themselves?

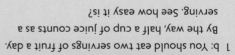

How do families affect health choices?

There's an old saying that goes, "You can pick your friends, but you can't pick your family." We don't get to choose our parents, grandparents, brothers, and sisters, but they have a big **influence** on how we turn out.

See if you can match these four people with their journal entries about their weekends.

Name: Hugh

Nickname: Huge

Likes: Things with wheels, watching cartoons, being with friends

Dislikes: Brussels sprouts, sitting still, silence

Favorite food: Spaghetti

Our sunny weekend

Because it was a sunny weekend, my dad, stepmother, and I went for a picnic. We took our bikes. We didn't go far, just to the park around the corner from their place. We had yummy, big, fat tuna sandwiches. I played at the playground while Dad and Gabby read the paper. After the ride, we went home and made pizza. We watched a movie after dinner.

On Sunday, we weeded the veggie garden and planted some herbs. Pa came around for lunch and then we all played Monopoly. I won!

Name: Jasmine

Nickname: Jazzy

Likes: Nature, making things, having fun

Dislikes: Noisy places, crowds, chewing gum

Favorite food: Chicken and mango salad

My weekend

My weekend was fun. Dad went to the football game with Uncle Mike on Saturday, so we girls went to aerobics with Mom. Then we went shopping. Mom wanted to buy a couple of new CDs for the dance class she teaches. Mom comes from Indonesia, and the local supermarket doesn't have all the great spices and herbs she uses in her cooking. So, we went to the Asian grocery store. I just love the way it smells in there.

On Sunday, Dad went to golf. My sister Jade and I watched some television, while Mom sewed sequins onto costumes. Jade and I invented some new dances and did each other's hair and makeup.

Just a weekend

Mom had to work on the weekend. On Saturday, Dad had some friends over to play cards. On Sunday, he wanted to watch television. He said I should find something to do with my sister, but she is such a pain. She talks all the time, and she always tries to tell me what to do. Our apartment is pretty small, and the only place I can get away from her is in my bedroom. She won't come in there because she says it's a **health hazard**!

So, I just sat around on my own, like I always do when Mom works on weekends—which is most of the time. When I got hungry, I came out and microwaved something, then took it back to my room. Nothing special happened.

Name: Saskia
Nickname: Sassy
Likes: Calisthenics, music, glitter, sleep-overs
Dislikes: Soccer, school shoes, cold weather
Favorite food: Satay beef

Our weekend

The weekend was unreal. My older brother was in a competition at the skate park on Saturday, so we all went to watch him. We rode our bikes there. Mom gets really nervous when she sees him getting air off the edge of the ramp. I think it's rad. Jarrod says he likes everything about skating except falling off! Ha ha!

On Sunday, Mom said she needed some time to herself, so Dad took Jarrod and me go-karting. It was cool. I think I'll have my birthday party there.

Name: Grant
Nickname: Grunt
Likes: Computer games, reading comics, a good laugh
Dislikes: The beach, anything green, getting sweaty
Favorite food: Hot dog with chili

Weekends are fun!

7

Can kids help improve adult health?

www.kidsincharge.com

Moonchick

Problem: Does anyone else out there have a parent who smokes? I just don't get it. I mean, there's a warning on the pack that says something like, "If you smoke these things, you'll die." But my dad just keeps right on puffing. He's tried to give up about a zillion times already. No luck. He smells. ☹ His car smells. ☹ It's disgusting. Plus, I don't want him to die. ☹ Any suggestions?

Helpppppp!

Moonchick

Cuddles

Hi Moonchick, gotta say I know exactly what you mean. I told my dad I'd never kiss or hug him again if he didn't quit. ♥ Worked great.

Ming

Good one, Cuddles. I tried hiding the pack and even broke the cigs in half. That just made him so annoyed that the smoke started coming out his ears! Plus I got a lecture about leaving other people's property alone. 👎

Startrooper

Hey Moonchick, why don't you just tell him how much you love him and how sad you'd be if he got sick—or even worse—died!

Indigo

My problem was my stepsister. She's 20 and plays guitar in a band. Way cool! 👍 All her friends smoke. Way uncool! Every day for a month, I printed out this picture of a smoker's lungs and stuck it on her mirror until she got the message.

Biscuits ~~(crossed out)~~   Rice crackers and corn thins would be good.
Dish soap
Bread   whole grain please!
Dog food
Cereal → Granola? Oatmeal?
Ice cream ~~(crossed out)~~ Yogurt?
Blank CD
Sunscreen for school

Shadow

Problem: Someone in my family always seems to be dieting. They eat whatever is in the house, and they don't go shopping very often. How do I get them to understand that if we had good food all the time they wouldn't need to keep dieting? I'm starving!

Aquaman

LOL! Shadow, I share your pain! Do they drink buckets of diet soda, but tell you to have water so you don't fill your body with chemicals? Mine do.

Kermit

Gee, my problem is a bit different. We have lots of food, but it's all the stuff my dad likes. He hates everything green, except grapes. I call it the white diet—white bread, potato, chicken, ice cream …

Griffon

Maybe you should all get a few books and pamphlets on the topic of healthy eating from the library or Internet. You could leave them around the house, and then give your families a homework assignment! Seriously, have you tried offering to go shopping with your parents so you can help them buy the right stuff? Or maybe help them do the shopping online?

Some adults might need help to remember how to have fun outside.

Some adults never forget how to play!

Did you know that lack of physical activity is a major reason adults become seriously ill?

9

Can advertising affect our choices?

Advertising tells us about what is available for us to buy and do. Sports teams use signs, local papers, and billboards to let us know where they are. The government gives us information about the dangers of drunk driving in advertising campaigns. We read, watch, and listen to advertisements every day. Do we always think about what they are encouraging us to do?

A super day

"What a beautiful morning," said Mom, gazing out the window above the kitchen sink. "Perfect for a picnic or a super-long bike ride—but I haven't forgotten. I promised you could choose what we'd do today. You've been so helpful while I did all that extra work. So what will it be?"

Deep down, I knew Mom wanted me to choose the picnic or the ride. But even deeper down, I wanted to go to the movies. All vacation I'd watched the ad on TV. It made me laugh every time I saw it. So I took a deep breath and admitted, "Well, you know that skateboarding movie I've been talking about? I sort of hoped we could go to see that."

"Well, if that's what you really want, Jamie, that's what we'll do."

"That's great, Mom." Then as I thought more about it, I started to feel guilty—for so many reasons. Now I'm not sure if I want to go to the movies.

Pester-Power

Have you ever heard the term "pester power"? This refers to the way children influence their parents when they nag, or pester, them to buy certain things. Kids often pester their parents to go to fast-food restaurants that give away toys with high-fat meals.

Active, slim, attractive people are used to advertise chocolate bars and energy drinks. "Eat this and you will have fun, be attractive, and have lots of energy!" Really? It is true that chocolate is a high-energy food, but most people eat chocolate when they are sitting down!

How much energy do you use watching television or reading a magazine? What happens to all that leftover energy from the chocolate bar?

On the other hand,

Sometimes we pause a little before we make a choice. We "look before we leap."

Life is full of choices, big and small, easy and hard, good and bad. Whenever we are faced with more than one thing to do, eat, or say, we have to choose. There are almost as many ways of choosing as there are choices to be made.

Sometimes we jump straight into things. We just go for it!

YES

NO

Sometimes we look at both sides of each choice before we decide. We weigh decisions.

Sometimes we just feel confused and don't know where to start.

Sometimes, we think so much about a choice, it becomes too hard to decide. We complicate things.

12

how do you choose?

Using thinking skills to make choices

You can use all sorts of thinking skills to help you make good health choices. Looking at both sides of a choice (the **positives** and the **negatives**) can be valuable. It leads you toward a balanced decision.

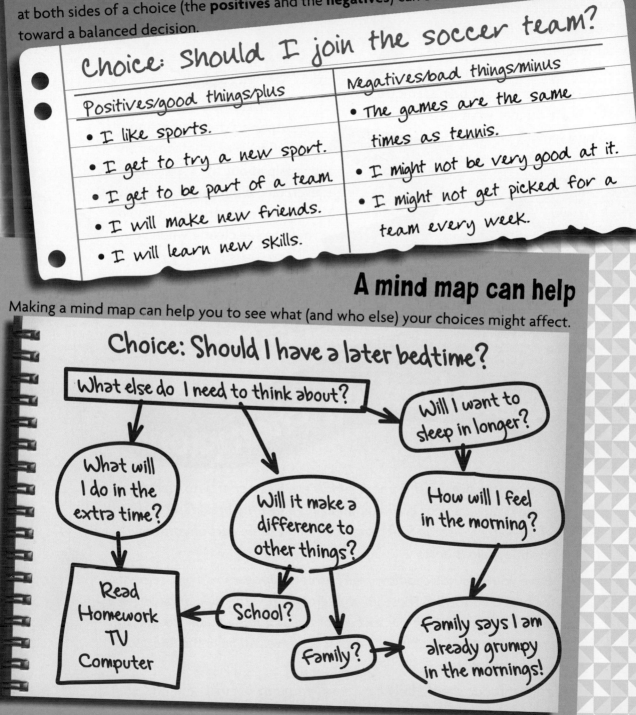

Choice: Should I join the soccer team?

Positives/good things/plus	Negatives/bad things/minus
• I like sports.	• The games are the same times as tennis.
• I get to try a new sport.	• I might not be very good at it.
• I get to be part of a team.	• I might not get picked for a team every week.
• I will make new friends.	
• I will learn new skills.	

A mind map can help

Making a mind map can help you to see what (and who else) your choices might affect.

Choice: Should I have a later bedtime?

What else do I need to think about?

- What will I do in the extra time? → Read Homework TV Computer
- Will it make a difference to other things? → School? / Family?
- Will I want to sleep in longer? → How will I feel in the morning? → Family says I am already grumpy in the mornings!

Do famous people affect our choices?

Who's your favorite singer? Favorite actor? Favorite athlete? If we are honest, we will all admit that, from time to time, we dream about being famous. We might wonder what it would be like to be a famous person. We might even try to be like one.

The **media** (magazines, radio, newspapers, television, and Web sites) give us information and gossip about the stars. Some of us even talk about famous people as if they were our friends. It can be hard to see clearly when you have stars in your eyes!

Breakfast of champions

A healthy breakfast is important. It gives you energy to start the day, and it powers your brain. What makes a healthy breakfast? It should have variety—some fruit, some dairy, and some **carbohydrates** (whole grain is best).

Have you ever noticed how many athletes appear in advertisements for breakfast foods? These advertisements link the idea of having a healthy breakfast with the success of the athletes we admire. We are supposed to think that if we eat that food we will have the energy to be a champion, too.

Breakfast foods should only have small amounts of sugar and fats. Don't forget to check the labels before deciding which cereal to choose!

Thin is in

The media is full of pictures of slim women. Sometimes, we spend more time talking about whether a star is too thin or too fat than we spend talking about how talented she might be!

When singer Mandisa Hundley competed on *American Idol*, one of the judges joked about her weight. Mandisa later lost over 80 pounds (36 kg).

What matters most, the size of the talent or the size of the dress?

Why do we expect actresses and singers to be thin?

What kind of thinker are you?

We all have different ways of looking at a problem or making a choice. The way we think is sometimes a bit like our **personalities**. If you know the characters in *Winnie the Pooh*, you will know that Eeyore is the gloomy one, Tigger is the cheerful one, and Piglet is the nervous one. The choices they make and the way they solve their problems are affected by their personalities and their outlooks on life.

Back in the 1980s, an expert on thinking, Edward de Bono, came up with a way to look at different types of thinking and thinkers. He invented the Six Thinking Hats. Each hat stands for a different way of thinking and each one is a different color.

We can change the way we think by imagining that we are wearing one of the hats. To make a careful decision, we can even try looking at it six different ways—six hats.

Do you think like any of the students in this example of a group at work?

Miss Watson looked at her watch. "Okay, class, you have ten minutes left to complete your 3-D puzzle." Group two was sitting by the window. Six students were crowded around one small table.

"This is just dumb! It's annoying. We'll never work this out!" Imogen growled, pushing her chair back so hard it nearly fell over. (Red hat thinking)

"Of course we will. We've almost got it. We just have to keep trying," said Fraser, encouragingly. (Yellow hat thinking)

"Are we looking at this the right way? Maybe we need to look at this in a different way," added Marlo. (Blue hat thinking)

"Hey, what happens if we turn it upside down?" Harley was tipping his head over so far to look at the puzzle that the spikes of his hair were touching the table. (Green hat thinking)

"That won't work. It would just wreck the bits we've already finished," Greta responded. (Black hat thinking)

"Let's think about what we've done so far. Maybe if we look at this step-by-step, we can work out what to do next," Willem suggested. (White hat thinking)

"You guys are almost there," Miss Watson commented, as she leaned over a very cranky-looking Imogen to open the window. "If you all try thinking like Willem, you might even be the first group to finish this challenge."

Six thinking hats

Green hat: Harley

Green hat thinking is about new ideas, imagination, and being creative. Remember, green is the color of fresh new leaves.

Yellow hat: Fraser

Yellow hat thinkers are positive. They look at the good things about a choice. This is sunny thinking.

White hat: Willem

White hat thinkers look just at the facts and information. A blank sheet of paper does not have an **opinion**.

Red hat: Imogen

Red hat thinking is based on your feelings and emotions. Remember, the color red stands for both love and anger. It is the color of the blood that runs through your body.

Black hat: Greta

Black hat thinkers look at the bad points. They focus on problems and weaknesses. This thinking can actually help you avoid making mistakes. The black of a dark night can be gloomy, but it can also be when you think ahead to tomorrow.

Blue hat: Marlo

Blue hat thinkers look down on a decision as if from above. They need to see the whole thing and think about what kind of thinking is needed! They look down from the blue sky.

Are you a team player?

Being fit and healthy helps us to feel good about ourselves. Joining a sports team or club can be a valuable part of this, but it is a choice that may not suit everyone.

Do you like to stand out or are you happiest in a group?

Sometimes one is the best number!

Some team activities rely on **individual** performances.

Cooperation is an important part of teamwork.

S says:
Forgot to ask today … R U going 2 try out 4 the basketball team 2morrow? I am. It would B fun 2 do 2gether.

H says:
MayB not 4 me. I'm not gr8 at b-ball plus G is on the team. G makes me nervous. I h8 how G hogs the ball & yells if NE1 makes a mistake.

S says:
Don't worry. Every1 thinks G is a pain. It's not just U. The new coach is cool. He listens 2 us & will sort it out. Pleeeeeeeeease come! We can pick U up on the way.

H says:
OK. You talked me in2 it. Thanx for Bing a good friend. C U then.

Have you read?

Soccer Hero by Matt Christopher

Baseball Great by Tim Green

What do young people think about team sports? A new survey reveals the answers.

A group of young people were surveyed on what they thought were the best (and worst) things about being involved in team sports. Here's what they said.

The "up" side of team sports

"The really great thing about being on a team is making friends. You all have something in common."

"I love being on a team because even when you lose, you still have each other."

"A lot of trusting and sharing goes on in teams. That makes me feel confident."

"Teamwork is definitely the best thing about team sports. You support each other."

"The members of a team can all be good at different things. You don't have to be great at playing all the positions to be a useful part of the team."

"Knowing I made a difference to our performance and getting praise from my team makes me feel good about myself."

The "down" side of team sports

"When someone in our class gets to pick a team, I'm always last to be chosen. It makes me feel embarrassed and ashamed."

"People who get too competitive and aggressive spoil the fun."

"If I miss a catch or something like that, I feel really bad, as if I've let down the rest of the team."

"It's really hard if you don't get picked for a big game, or if you sit on the bench for ages waiting to get out there and play."

"I don't really like team sports because of the pressure other people put on me. I like to set my own challenges."

It seems that the survey has found positives and negatives about being involved in team sports. It is up to everyone to consider what is the best activity or sport to undertake.

What is a wise choice?

Have you ever really wanted something—wanted it so badly that you were willing to do almost anything to have it? When we feel like that, we don't care about being wise. We don't want to be sensible; we just want to satisfy our desires. Those are the times when we do not make our best choices.

Things in our **environment**, such as how much time, money, and space we have, can limit our choices. Things about ourselves can also be limiting—our age, size, and health conditions matter.

City living

Are your dreams bigger than your body can manage?

Do you understand the saying, "You have to walk before you can run"?

To help make a wise choice, we need to ask ourselves some questions:

- What do I really want?
- Why do I really want it?
- Is it a realistic choice or is it just a dream?

BIRTHDAY WISH LIST.

PONY—a palomino would be nice

BIKE and HELMET—
favorite color: red

CANOE—not fussy about color

Have you thought about the time involved? Does your weekly schedule have a balance of activities?

Do you want to play the game, or is it something else you really want?

When was the last time you tried something new or something you didn't like when you were younger?

You are often faced with choices. It is important to remember that, as you get older, things change. Your body changes as you grow. Your ideas and opinions grow, too. Even your tastes change!

You might find you like something you used to dislike. It's okay to change your mind. Change can be very healthy.

21

Can friends influence health choices?

Friends are an important part of our lives. True friends share good times and bad. They really care about each other. Feeling like you belong and have friends to have fun with is one of the healthiest feelings in the world.

Friends care for each other.

Friends support and help each other. They encourage us when we are nervous. Sometimes, the need to belong is what makes us try new things. Have you ever been invited to try a great new activity with friends—bowling, surfing, horseback riding, in-line skating, rock climbing?

Friends share good and bad times.

Friends try new things together.

Perhaps you thought you didn't like something (such as hiking, a sport, or even a new food such as sushi) until you tried it with a friend or at a friend's house. Doing new things with friends not only gives us more experiences, it also helps us feel confident.

At other times, the need to belong might lead us to make bad decisions. We might even do something that makes us feel uncomfortable or unsafe. Nobody likes to feel left out, but it is important to think about what you are doing. Remember, you have the right to say, "This might not be such a great idea. I don't want to do it."

Friends respect each other's decisions.

Friends are never left out.

Friends support and help each other.

Have you read?

Hit and Run by Dawn Hunter and Karen Hunter

Girls Got Game: Sports Stories and Poems by Sue Macy

Jackie Robinson: Champion for Equality by Michael Teitelbaum

What if there's really no choice?

There are times when the choices about what's best for your health are not in your control.

Sticky Medicine Goo

"No school today,"
I heard my dad say.
"She can stay where she is in her bed.
With that cold in her chest,
she can stay there and rest
so it doesn't sneak up to her head."

Oh well, that's okay.
There's a math test today
that I didn't want to do.
I'll be happier here,
but there's just one thing I fear—
they'll smear me with medicine goo!

Those fumes up my nose,
sleeping cat at my toes,
and the covers pulled up to my chin.
Sticky medicine goo on my chest,
I smell weird but not stressed.
Tomorrow I'll tell my cold, "I win!"

WHAT'S ON YOUR PLATE?

When you eat your dinner,
it's best to take great care.
All sorts of strange things
might be lurking there.

You may discover parsnips, peas,
or even brussels sprouts
are lurking near the carrots
or somewhere thereabouts.

They might be under gravy
or hidden by a spud
or mixed in with the casserole,
like rotting leaves in mud.

Some things you can eat at once,
and other things must wait.
Some you cannot eat at all
but push around the plate.

So always be most cautious
eating your dinner—each bite.
You may find some weird stuff
actually tastes...alright!

Does every health choice count?

Every day, we make hundreds of little decisions that can affect our health. Things that don't seem important today might matter tomorrow. Little things can add up to become big things.

Do I have time to wash my hands? I'm in a hurry.

Do you have time to get sick?

I wish I'd cleaned my teeth properly!

Labels tell us exactly what is in the food we buy. Take time to read the labels.

The **germs** that cause diseases are so tiny we cannot see them. A sneeze can spread thousands of germs for more than 2 yards (2 m) around you. Your sneeze might be the fastest thing about you! Some sneezes blast germs out at almost 90 miles (145 km) per hour!

"Last week I forgot to take my hat to school. It was a sunny day, but I didn't think it would matter too much. Of course, we're not allowed to play in the sun without a hat, but our teacher keeps a spare one in the classroom. So I just wore that. Well, guess what? The person who wore it before me had head lice!"

Go ahead, enjoy the hot dog or pie. Just remember to balance it with lots of vegetables later on. Don't forget to exercise as well.

How much sleep is healthy?

Age	Hours of sleep needed per day
0–2 months	10.5–18.5
2–12 months	13.0–15.0
1–3 years	12.0–14.0
3–5 years	11.0–14.0
5–12 years	9.5–11.0

Sunglasses protect your eyes from damage by ultraviolet (UV) radiation. They're like sunscreen for your eyes!

Good hygiene is part of having self-respect.

You choose chocolate. It doesn't choose you!

Where do you find good advice?

All choices are personal. We need to be able to make our own decisions, but there are times when we need help. It is important to know how and where to find good advice. When it comes to your health and well-being, you need to be sure your choices are wise and well-informed.

Helen's number-one tip: Get good information and ask someone you trust.

Finding help at school!

Helen is a **counselor** at a school. Her job is to counsel students with problems and guide them in healthy living.

"Naturally, I don't have all the answers," says Helen. "Who does? But I can at least point people in the right direction. I help them find help!"

Nobody can make a wise choice if they do not have all the information—the whole picture.

"As I see it," Helen explains, "there are four main ways to find information for making a healthy choice. You can talk about it, read about it, watch someone else do it, or try it yourself.

"If you were looking for a way to deal with a serious health issue, such as a weight problem, it would be different. You can't really watch someone else, and it can be dangerous to try diets by yourself. You need advice from a health professional like your family doctor.

"The best person to talk to is someone who knows more about the topic than you, someone with experience. That might be a member of your family, a teacher, a coach, a medical expert, a member of your religious community, or even a specialist like a **dietician**."

Your friends might not be quite expert enough!

Older people have a lot of experience to share with you.

Ask someone you trust

There are risks with contacting people on the Internet or calling people you do not know. Be very careful. However, there are organizations that are set up just to help kids. One of those is the Boys Town Hotline.

The Boys Town National Hotline is a free and confidential 24-hour counseling service for all American and Canadian kids, teens, and parents.

Since 1989, Boys Town has been listening to young people talk about a wide range of issues both big and small. Kids can call about everything from everyday topics (family, friends, and school) to more serious issues (**child abuse**, bullying, mental health, drug and alcohol use, homelessness, and suicide).

Counseling is available over the phone (1-800-448-3000) or via e-mail. Check out www.boystown.org.

Information from reading can really stack up!

Be careful when on the Internet. Not all of the information out there is reliable.

29

Do your choices affect others?

Every decision has an impact. Of course, a decision affects the person who makes it—you. Your choice might move you into a new area of your life, such as taking up a different sport or joining a club. It might also bring a chapter of your life to an end. You might give up tennis lessons to play soccer, for example.

Life choices can have an impact on those around you, too. How do your decisions affect them?

Family and friendship groups are a big part of our lives. We should consider them when we make big decisions.

Supporting someone's health choice might mean watching them play a sport.

Glossary

advertising campaign	a series of advertisements to make people aware of something
balanced diet	meals that are made up of the best combination of healthy foods
carbohydrates	substances in foods such as sugar, pasta, and bread that provide your body with heat and energy
child abuse	cruel or hurtful treatment of a young person
counselor	a person whose job is to give advice to others and help them make wise decisions
dietician	a person who works as a food expert, giving advice about what to eat
environment	the people and things around you in your life
germs	tiny living things that cause disease
health hazard	something that is dangerous to good health
hygiene	being clean to stay healthy
individual	one person; single and different
influence	something that can cause change
media	television, newspapers, magazines, and the Internet
negatives	the bad side of things
opinion	what a person thinks or believes about something
personalities	individuals' own special qualities and ways of behaving
positives	the good side of things

For Further Information

Books

Kajander, Rebecca, and Timothy Culbert. *Be Fit, Be Strong, Be You.* Minneapolis: Free Spirit Publishing, 2010.

Miller, Edward. *The Monster Health Book: A Guide to Eating Healthy, Being Active & Feeling Great for Monsters & Kids!* New York: Holiday House, 2006.

Web Sites

Don't Buy It! Get Media Smart
pbskids.org/dontbuyit/advertisingtricks/

Health and Safety: Health Issues
www.kids.gov/k_5/k_5_health_issues.shtml

Publisher's note to educators and parents: Our editors have carefully reviewed these Web sites to ensure that they are suitable for students. Many Web sites change frequently, however, and we cannot guarantee that a site's future contents will continue to meet our high standards of quality and educational value. Be advised that students should be closely supervised whenever they access the Internet.

Index